Perfect
Stress
Control

THE PERFECT SERIES

ALL YOU NEED TO GET IT RIGHT FIRST TIME

Perfect Stress Control

ALL YOU NEED
TO GET IT RIGHT
FIRST TIME

Carole McKenzie

ARROW
BUSINESS BOOKS

Published by Arrow Books in 1994

1 3 5 7 9 10 8 6 4 2

© Carole McKenzie 1994

Carole McKenzie has asserted her right under the Copyright,
Designs and Patents Act, 1988, to be identified as the author of this
work.

First published by
Arrow Books Limited
20 Vauxhall Bridge Road, London SW1V 2SA

Random House Australia (Pty) Limited
20 Alfred Street, Milsons Point, Sydney
New South Wales 2061, Australia

Random House New Zealand Limited
18 Poland Road, Glenfield
Auckland 10, New Zealand

Random House South Africa (Pty) Limited
PO Box 337, Bergvlei, South Africa

Random House UK Limited Reg. No. 954009

ISBN 0-09-937941-4

Set in Bembo by
SX Composing Ltd., Rayleigh, Essex
Printed and bound in Great Britain by
Cox and Wyman Ltd, Reading, Berks

ABOUT THE AUTHOR

Carole McKenzie is a director of Communication and Integrity Works, a company specializing in presentation skills and business ethics training. She is a member of the Institute of Training and Development, and author of three books on speaking in public, as well as a number of books in the 'Quotable' series.

A former teacher, she later moved into training, and for some years was training and development specialist for a large multi-national company.
She is currently working on several books, including her first novel, and is in her final year of study at the London Academy of Graphology.

As a working woman and mother she is aware of the many stressful situations which can arise at home and work. As a Scot, she is certain that thorough preparation is a good starting point for perfect stress control.

For information on all our services, please call:
071 938 2025 or 0344 777203

CONTENTS

INTRODUCTION

> **'The human brain starts the moment we are born and never stops until we stand up to speak in public.'**
>
> George Jessel

This is one of my favourite quotations, and one with which anybody who has ever had to make a speech will empathize. Many business people today could substitute 'speaking in public' for many other management situations. For example, you may feel stressed when asked to conduct an interview or even to take part in a business meeting. With a few simple 'management techniques' anyone can reduce their stress level, no matter what the situation.

The overall theme of this book is stress. Stress can have many causes, and negative stress can prevent us from performing at our very best. I believe that one of the main reasons for stress at work is lack of preparation.

90% PREPARATION 10% PERSPIRATION

Many management topics are covered comprehensively under separate headings in the PERFECT series. The topic of this book is **Stress and how to minimize it** in a number of familiar management situations.

As well as general tips on time management (poor time management is often cited as a common cause of stress), useful checklists are given on preparation for each topic.

> **'The bow too tensely strung is easily broken.'**
>
> Publius Syrus (1st century BC)

Research into work-related stress in Europe and the United States shows that many of the following issues have been found to be particularly stressful in large organizations.

Relationships	Inability to get on with people, conflict with superiors, colleagues.
Role in organization	No definite role specification, lack of clear objectives, difficulty in delegation, poor time management.
Organizational factors	No positive feedback on performance, no acceptance of new ideas, poor communications, threat of redundancy.
Imposed restraints	Rapid change. Unrealistic targets, high work load, head count restrictions, reduced training budgets, unchosen teams. Need to 'perform' at meetings, presentations, interviews.

Stress affects both men and women. Please read he as he/she.

STRESS – WHAT IS IT?

We all know what stress feels like, whether we call it pressure, panic, anxiety or tension. We all get it, whether it's the thought of standing up to present a report at a board meeting, or the mere thought of driving down the motorway to attend a client presentation. We have all heard colleagues, for example, say 'I just can't cope with all this paperwork', or, 'Things are getting on top of me.' A common complaint I hear from clients is, 'I just don't have time to prepare a thorough presentation.'

Life without stress would be no life at all. All change is stressful, but it is only by standing back from the situation and analyzing it clearly that we can see exactly why we react as we do, and how we can stop the damage caused.

It is possible to learn new ways of thinking and working which will help reduce stress. If you are a business man or woman, you will almost certainly recognize the people and situations which follow. I hope that most or all of you will recognize yourself. Often identifying a potential stressor is the first step to stress control.

There are no formulae for living a stress-free life, and this book is not a recipe for 'how to live'. The objective of this book is rather to help you identify business situations where you may feel you could make improvements; to make them more enjoyable and less stressful.

At a stress management conference in 1989 stress was defined as:

High Demands plus High Constraints, plus Low Support = Stress

It is clear that this definition can be seen as both an individual and an organizational issue.

The first step towards stress reduction is to admit to yourself that you are already suffering stress, or are a potential candidate. The following is a list of symptoms which may indicate stress. The higher the number of symptoms you recognize, the more urgent the need to look at your lifestyle and work practices. The list is limited to the ten most commonly reported:

SYMPTOMS

Physical

- Palpitations and breathlessness

- Stomach cramps
- Headaches
- Unexplained aches and pains
- Constipation or diarrhoea
- Dry mouth
- Shaking limbs
- Nausea
- Excessive sweating
- Alteration of menstrual pattern in women.

Emotional

- Loss of concentration
- Worry
- Irritability
- Lack of self-esteem
- Loss of confidence
- Feeling apprehensive
- Loss of enthusiasm
- Cynicism
- Unhappiness, loss of sense of humour
- Feelings of dissatisfaction.

Behavioural

- Over indulgence in food/smoking/alcohol
- Dependence on drugs
- Changes in sleep patterns: difficulty dropping off, waking early, waking tired
- Being too busy to take time off for hobbies/holidays/exercise
- Taking work home
- Difficulty in making decisions
- Consistently working late
- Poor time management
- Loss of appetite or major weight loss/gain
- A shut down of emotions and loss of interest in everyday events. Tears near to surface for no apparent reason.

STRESS RATING

Psychologists have compiled a list of some of life's stressful events and given each a score. If your total in any 12-month period exceeds 75 points, you have a 50/50 chance of a stress-related illness. For a total of 150 points, the chance of developing a stress-related illness soars to 80/20. Use the figures below to give your own score to events not listed but which you find stressful.

Stress Rating

- Death/bereavement   50
- Separation/divorce   35
- Moving House   31
- Marriage   25
- Redundancy/retirement   23
- Pregnancy/care for elderly   20
- Changes at work   18
- Family squabbles   17
- Promotion   16
- Change in lifestyle   13
- Changed working conditions   10
- New hobby/social life   9
- Changing sleep patterns   8
- Change in diet or eating habit   7
- Holidays/Christmas   6
- A brush with the law   5

Not all stress is bad for us and not all stressful events have the same effect on people. It is the intangible nature of the condition that makes it so difficult to recognize and conquer.

The following are some questions to ask about your working environment.

STRESS IN THE WORK ENVIRONMENT

Possible Causes of Stress at Work
Work

- Do you consistently meet deadlines?
- Do you have an opportunity to take short breaks during the day?
- Is your work sufficiently interesting and varied?
- Do you have enough work to do?

Feelings about your work

- Do you feel that your job is worthwhile?
- Do you feel that what you do is appreciated by others?
- Do you have a choice of daily work pattern?

Colleagues

- Do you enjoy working with your colleague?
- Can you discuss work-related problems with them?

Your manager

- Do you get feedback on your work?
- Does he give you constructive criticism/praise when warranted?
- Does your manager operate an open-door policy?
- Do you discuss your career planning with him?

Your role within the organization

- Do you have a job description?
- Do you have clear objectives?
- Are you kept informed of changes in the company which affect your job?
- Do you have sufficient resources to do your job successfully?
- Are you fairly paid for the job?

Environment

- Is your workplace conducive to the work you do there?
- Is your workplace well laid out, well lit, adequately ventilated, comfortably heated?
- Do you have your own desk/work station?
- Do you have sufficient privacy?

A common factor which I have noticed over the last few years is the increased stress levels being experienced by working women. In the 1990s women are encouraged to be the 'perfect mother', the 'perfect manager'. They often place unrealistic expectations on themselves at home and at work, and if there is little support from their employer, the outcome may result in stress. Fortunately most responsible organizations operate an Equal Opportunity Policy, and are sensitive to issues of sexism and racism. They also encourage training.

At the end of this exercise, you may have highlighted several major sources of stress at work.

Causes of negative stress

- Not getting enough success – leading to low self-esteem
- Different attitudes/values from boss
- Impossible deadlines imposed without consultation
- Colleagues being made redundant
- Inadequate resources to do a good job
- Facing up to situations which have been avoided and therefore never having learned to cope with them
- Power struggles – winning is fun, losing is not
- Personal: divorce, ill health, moving house etc.

It is as well to recognize that there are some things we can't change, short of looking for another job. However, some of the above most-complained-about aspects of work could certainly be improved. For example, many of the questions about work, meeting deadlines and work patterns, could be improved with better time management.

Some of the factors under **Work Environment** could be improved with a little planning.

I often advise Presentation Skills clients to 'claim' the stage or floor space in front of the audience, and to 'make it their own'. This might simply consist of personalizing it and giving some thought to their preferred work style – for example to stand behind a table, or remove it altogether; if using a flip chart or demonstration equipment, to ask themselves – 'where do I feel comfortable standing/sitting?' Remember if you feel comfortable, you will look comfortable, and therefore less stressed.

Try:

- Moving your desk and other office equipment to another position
- Clearing your desk of all paperwork. Have only the work in progress on the desk. Allocate a file drawer for the rest of the paperwork, to be tackled later
- Surrounding yourself with things to lift your spirits. For example, plants, flowers, posters, photographs
- If you need to work undisturbed, without the normal office hubbub of interruptions and telephones, remove yourself to a quiet room. Most offices have a board room, training or interview room which is not in constant use. Trying to work with constant interruptions is a major cause of stress.

Your Workspace
Take an objective look at your work space

		Yes	No
1.	Does your desk grow paper?	_____	_____
2.	Is your desk a clean working surface that helps you focus your energy on the task in hand?	_____	_____
3.	Do you get a positive feeling when you approach your desk?	_____	_____
4.	Is your desk such a mess that you invent ways to avoid it all together?	_____	_____
5.	Is your filing cabinet a black hole that sucks in paper, notes, articles, documents and endless items you have duplicated?	_____	_____
6.	Is your filing system a streamlined, orderly one that supports you in getting your job done?	_____	_____
7.	Is the physical appearance of your work space uncluttered, cheerful and light?	_____	_____
8.	Is your work space conducive to clear, creative thinking?	_____	_____

Managing your manager

'If you don't know where you are going you'll end up somewhere else.'

One of the commonest complaints from employees is that they are not quite sure what they should be doing. In other words, they have no job description or objectives. This lack of direction and feedback feeds feelings of anxiety. Check that:

● You have a current job description. If you don't,

then liaise with your Manager or Personnel Department to write one
- You have up-to-date objectives for your job
- Your objectives are in writing
- You understand and have agreed these with your manager
- You know the performance factors relating to your objectives.

Managing your career

- Set goals for yourself. Ask, what do I want to be doing one year from now? In five years?
- Discuss career prospects with your manager. Performance appraisal time is a good opportunity to start (See Chapter 9)
- Assess what training (if any) you need to develop the skills/knowledge which are holding you back
- Draw up an outline plan to put you back in the driving seat
- Put realistic time frames on it.

Often poor communication is a cause of stress at work. Many employees complain that they never get 'positive strokes' from their managers. Here are ten suggestions for getting along better with people:

1. Think before you speak. Say less than you think.
2. Make promises sparingly, and always keep them.
3. Never let an opportunity pass to give praise or say a kind word. Give credit where it is due.
4. Show interest in others, their work, hobbies, families.
5. Be cheerful and adopt a positive attitude. Don't dwell on the negative.
6. Discourage gossip, and don't take part in it. It is destructive.

7. Be careful of other people's feelings.
8. Disregard any ill-natured remarks about you. Live so that nobody will believe them.
9. Don't be anxious about getting credit. Just do your best and be patient.
10. Keep an open mind. Discuss but don't argue. Try to put yourself in other people's shoes.

Scientific research shows clearly that certain emotions and states of mind can exert enormous influence on our long-term mental and physical health. For example if you're feeling stressed, this can cause an increased heart rate and rise in blood pressure. Clinical evidence has shown that the stress of anger produces a unique hormonal response that is particularly dangerous to your health. This doesn't mean the occasional angry outburst which helps clear the air, but anger of the chronic, sustained variety. This state can lead to symptoms such as hypertension, digestive disorders, skin complaints, rashes, headaches and heart disease. One American study carried out over a 25-year period found that the 20 per cent of respondents who scored highest on a hostility ratings scale all died earlier than those whose hostility readings were much lower.

Anger works by blocking unpleasant sensations caused by stressful events. The positive side of anger is that it can often mobilize you to make changes in your life which, if you didn't feel quite so riled, you would never consider. If your anger does get out of control, try one of the following:

Action

- Verbalize what you feel. Calmly talk it through with the person responsible
- Keep an anger diary. Note down all the situations in

which you feel angry – this should highlight prob-
lem areas
- Exercise is often the solution to expending angry
energy
- Use relaxation techniques
- Humour can help put things in perspective.

Strengthening your working relationship

*How to increase your staff's sense of well-being and
enhance their self-esteem*

Catch your staff doing something right! People who
produce good results feel good about themselves.

*How to establish a good working relationship with
your staff*

- Smile
- Establish eye contact
- Use their names
- Give your undivided attention
- Mirror and pace their body language, etc.
- Try to 'speak the same language'
- Show that, without any shadow of doubt, you re-
spect and accept the person, regardless of race, sex,
culture etc.
- Demonstrate respect for your colleagues and your
organization
- Be calm and confident
- Be well-groomed and look the part.

1

LOW STRESS COMMUNICATING

STRESS IS A CHAIN REACTION

You will find it beneficial if you can help employees and colleagues keep their own stress levels down. This will help everyone to work more productively. A good rule of thumb is to try to make as many of your transactions rewarding and positive for the other people involved. Experience tells us that this is not always possible, as there are times when you need to take a strong position in opposition to others.

Think about your own personal communication style with others. Is it, in behavioural science terminology, a punishing experience, i.e. one that an individual is not likely to repeat? Or is it a rewarding experience, i.e. one that he is likely to want to have again. If the people with whom you communicate usually experience their transactions with you as positive, affirming to their own self-esteem, and productive for them personally, **they will usually repeat the experience**. If they don't like the result, **they will interact with you as little as possible.**

This principle provides a very simple way to assess your communication skills and to identify specific managerial behaviours that cause stress to others. Review your day-to-day communication patterns of communicating with others in work and non-work situations. Ask yourself the question, 'To what extent do people seek me out – to communicate with me, share ideas, include me in their personal and social activities?'

This may seem such an obvious point as not to deserve mentioning. The reality is that so many people who work together in organizations don't seem to grasp it at all. Many can keep it in mind only under pleasant circumstances, and forget it when the pressure is on. Stress is a chain reaction, specific managerial behaviours can cause stress for others as well as yourself.

The following are some of the most common **punishing behaviours**:

- Monopolizing the conversation
- Displaying negative body language
- Insulting or using non-verbal put-downs
- Speaking dogmatically; not respecting others' opinions
- Criticizing excessively; fault finding
- Refusing to negotiate or compromise
- Playing 'games' with people; manipulating or competing in subtle ways
- Overusing 'should' language
- Asking loaded or accusing questions
- Breaking confidences
- Failing to keep promises.

Rewarding behaviours include:

- Giving others a chance to express views, share opinions and information.
- Listening attentively
- Displaying positive body language
- Giving constructive feedback
- Negotiating
- Treating others as equals
- Stating one's needs and desires honestly
- Confronting others constructively on difficult issues
- Questioning others openly and honestly
- Keeping the confidences of others
- Giving one's word sparingly and keeping it

- Expressing genuine interest in the other person
- Keeping a sense of humour.

Review these lists and add any other behaviours that come to mind. Think about your own personal style and see which specific behaviours you can identify in your day-to-day patterns of working with others. Decide whether your management style is that of a punisher or a rewarder. These behaviours also apply in private life.

In the long term, it is the rewarding style of dealing with others that helps keep down your own stress levels; it helps others do the same, and makes life more pleasant for everyone. Building constructive, congenial relationships with others helps to minimize your over-all stress, but also can play a direct part in your career success and in your advancement in the organization.

A PROBLEM OR A CHALLENGE?
How we view stressful events has an effect on how we cope with them. Often it helps to deal with the situation step by step. Try this five point plan:

1. Define the problem.
2. Brainstorm a wide range of alternative actions for dealing with the problem. (Consider how your colleagues might tackle it.)
3. Look at your list and evaluate the pros and cons of each idea. Rank them in order of most practical.
4. Try the most acceptable and feasible solution.
5. Reconsider the original problem in the light of your attempts to tackle it. How does it look now?

To tackle the problem in this way you will need time to sit quietly and work out your strategy; you will need to speak to other people about it, get their advice, and en-list their support.

Exposing yourself to small amounts of stress at a time helps you to focus in on the problem, a little at a time. Very often we get into 'stress overload' when we look at the 'whole picture', which looks too much to handle, and we may be tempted to give up. This only serves to increase stress levels.

2

THEMES FOR REDUCING STRESS

BEING ASSERTIVE

- Don't apologise profusely
- Be direct
- Keep it short
- Don't justify yourself for making the request
- Give a reason for the request (Don't try to 'sell' it.)
- Don't play on people's friendship or good nature
- Don't take a refusal personally
- Respect the other person's right to say no.

Refusing requests

- Keep it short
- Keep it simple
- Give a reason – but don't invent an excuse
- Avoid 'I can't' phrases
- Don't apologise profusely
- Pay acknowledgement to the requester: 'Thank you, but . . .'
- Honestly state limitations: 'It will be impossible to . . . but I could . . .'
- Ask for clarification, more information, or time to decide
- Speak steadily and calmly.

TIME MANAGEMENT AND ANXIETY

Among the skills needed by today's executives/managers is the capacity to work comfortably under pressure. The following five categories have been identified as contributing to the relationship between poor time management and anxiety:

- Thoughts and feelings of inadequacy, including self-criticism or self-condemnation, such as calling oneself names like 'stupid'
- Worrying about one's performance, as compared with personal standards or how well others are doing
- Contemplating alternatives – too long and fruitlessly
- Thinking about imagined consequences of doing poorly in the test – disapproval, punishment, loss of status or self-esteem, damage to academic record or career prospects
- Being preoccupied with bodily reactions associated with anxiety, leading to intensified anxiety symptoms.

Here are a few steps towards capturing a positive state of mind to cope:

1. Realize that pressure can be handled without discomfort.
2. Analyze the pressure you feel and prepare for similar situations in the future.
3. Anticipate deadlines – start early.
4. Find a hobby that relaxes you.
5. Say 'no'.
6. Work no more than ten hours daily.
7. Examine your eating patterns and balance your diet.
8. Plan some time for yourself every day.

Stress results from the anticipation of future unpleasantness, especially unpleasantness that we feel we may not be able to cope with. And our time management suffers. The person who moves from one current demand to another without systematically assessing and planning for future outcomes will be less certain about how to handle future demands. The following are some helpful hints for improving your self-organization.

Key ideas for better time management

1. List goals and set priorities. (Remember to set clear objectives.)
2. Make a daily 'To do' list.
3. Start with your top priority on the list. (Work down your list, from most important to least important.)
4. Ask 'What is the best use of my time right now?'
5. Handle each piece of paper only once.
6. Don't procrastinate – do it now!

Here are a few of the most common problems facing managers and some suggested solutions.

Problem
Task is unpleasant/difficult/risky, for example preparing a report or presentation giving bad news.

Possible solution
Give yourself a pep talk: 'Next time I pick this up, I'll do something about it.' This is a start. If guilt is getting in the way, put aside time to address the deeper issues so that you get yourself into a positive frame of mind.

Problem
You started the job, got bogged down and couldn't restart.

Possible solution
Try one of these:

- Before you stop, have the next step planned
- Take a break
- Try new surroundings

- Stand up if you have been sitting
- If the task is repetitious, set yourself 'mini' dead-lines to meet
- Award yourself a 'treat' when you have met your deadlines, e.g. buy yourself a book, flowers, a new tie
- arrange the task differently.

Problem

You have an unpleasant priority task to start and are about to start on a non-priority task.

Possible solution

Ask yourself what you are afraid of:

- getting angry?
- feeling guilty?
- hurting yourself or a colleague?
- being rejected?
- taking on too much responsibility?

Now, write down what you are afraid of. Single out your most likely concern and deal with that head on, e.g. if you write the procedure manual, will you do yourself out of a job?

Problem

You haven't got the resources to do the kind of job you would like to feel proud of.

Possible solution

Don't aim for perfection, just do the best you can – but discuss it with your boss and get his acknowledgement, at least about acceptable quality standards.

Planning time

Identifying time stealers

The following are six of the most often quoted time-stealers for business people.

1. Answering the telephone
2. Dealing with mail
3. Attending meetings
4. Paperwork
5. Commuting
6. Business lunches.

You need to examine how your time is spent. Memory itself is very misleading. A time sheet, diary, log, etc. will provide reliable information. Keep a log for a month. This will enable you to identify and eliminate things that need not be done at all. Ask the question, 'What would happen if this were not done at all?' If the answer is 'nothing', there's not much point in wasting time doing it. We waste a lot of time in routine tasks, for example, paper work.

Next to the dog the wastebasket is man's best friend.

B.C. Forbes

There may appear to be unlimited ways in which a piece of paper can be dealt with, and that can lead to painful and unnecessary dithering over fairly unimportant correspondence. In fact there is a mercifully limited choice of actions when confronted with any document. Start today to separate your mail and deal with it in these simple ways:

- Throw it away
- Pass it on
- File it
- Clip it into the workbook.

If you decide to file, then decide who will file what and for how long.

Five tips for easy filing

1. Put the more recent information in the front of folders.
2. Staple papers together, don't clip. Clips fall off or tangle the paper.
3. Lightly pencil in 'throwaway dates' on filed material.
4. Fold oversized papers with the printing on the outside for easy reading.
5. Don't leave papers lying around randomly – **Don't pile, file**.

Why not clip a copy of this simple list of options to your in-tray as a reminder?

LEARN TO PLAN

Without planning it is impossible to predict, prepare for and cope with the future. It is just as important for individuals to plan as it is for large organizations. The future arrives whether we are ready for it or not. Being able to anticipate and meet the demands of the future means one is less vulnerable to stress. There are three major planning steps:

*   Selection of goals
*   Formulating objectives from goals
*   Selection of the activities for the achievement of objectives.

To begin, ask yourself the question 'What do I want out of life?' Start answering this question in terms of broad, general categories. Think of all the things you would like to achieve, obtain, or experience and list them. List everything, even those areas that are not realistic without prioritizing. For example:

Career goals

1. Gain promotion

2. Increase quota
3. Study for an MBA
4. Build skills by attending management training courses
5. Start own business.

Personal

1. Wealth
2. A good relationship
3. Sail around the world
4. Write a book
5. Own a Porche
   and so on . . .

Once you have generated your list, go back and examine it. Look for goals that are not likely to be within your power. Some may be modified to more achievable ones.

Try to be clear about what you mean by each goal statement. The clearer and more specific the goal, the easier it is to decide whether it is achievable. If you feel it is possible, think about how you would go about it.

Look for inconsistencies among your goals. Working toward incompatible goals can tear you apart psychologically. Examples of some common pairs of goals that are inconsistent in most cases are the following:

● Attain career advancement and never work evenings and weekends
● Have strong opinions, speak your mind, and still have everyone like you.

Spotting conflicting goals will alert you to potential problems.

Rank-order the goals
Earlier in this book we looked at setting clear objectives. The same rules apply here. Decide which goals

are most important to you, then derive a set of objectives for each one. Make them specific. For example, number 4 goal, to write a book, will involve many steps, each with an objective. The following may form the preliminary steps before you actually start writing:

- Research: subject, market, publishers
- Decide theme – write synopsis for publisher
- Submit synopsis to publisher etc.

It is clear that these are very broad outlines that need to be broken down. For example, under research, the first objective might be: 'By the 3rd of this month, all subject research will be completed.' Setting objectives enables us to break up our larger and more unwieldy goals into smaller, more manageable pieces. Putting a time on objectives also helps us to keep tabs on progress. Tasks under this objective may include visiting the library, reading books and publishers brochures, and visiting bookshops.

The final stage of all objective setting is recording and appraising progress.

Record progress
An appointment book, which breaks the day into half-hour blocks, is useful for recording progress.

- Record the objective and activities related to the goal you wish to achieve
- Allocate times for those activities and write them in your weekly schedule
- Check these daily/weekly to assess progress and adjust as necessary.

The following acronym should help you to remember to include all the elements of good objectives in future:

Good objectives should be SMART

This means:

Specific	– Clear and unambiguous
Measurable	– How will you know you have achieved them?
Agreed	– With you. (You must 'buy into' the idea and want to succeed.)
Realistic	– Achievable
Timely	– Can be done in the time available

Procrastination

Procrastination, or putting off things that you want or need to do, goes hand in hand with stress and poor time management. Ultimately, avoidance breeds avoidance. Avoiders fall farther and farther behind and the work mounts up.

To help avoid procrastination, you may have to look at your working methods. For example, some of the following factors actually help us procrastinate.

Perfectionism

Being a perfectionist makes one more likely also to be a procrastinator. As a perfectionist, you are dissatisfied unless you do things perfectly. You always feel something of a failure if any performance has a flaw. Therefore any task becomes aversive, because no task is ever completed 100 per cent right. Like the manager who puts off writing his report until the night before it is due – by which time it is too late for him to produce the high-calibre work he is capable of.

Inappropriate commitments

In order to do those things in life that are really important to you, you must learn to make appropriate commitments. Most of us are more likely to honour a commitment made to another person than we are to honour a commitment made to ourselves. This is a fact we can turn either to our advantage or disadvantage.

If you are the kind of person who says 'Yes' to most requests made on your time by other people, you are likely to be someone who often does not get around to doing the things that are important to you.

To achieve your own goals, you must learn to avoid commitments that waste your time. Conversely, making a commitment to others (especially a public commitment) to do something that is important to you is an excellent way to mobilize yourself.

Deception

Another way to procrastinate is by self-deception. **Straightforward procrastination** is, for example, going to the theatre when you need to be planning for presentation to the Board. **Devious procrastination** involves performing some activity other than the target activity because (1) it is redeeming in some way, or (2) it is 'preparation' for the target activity. Reading a book entitled 'Conducting Meetings' when you need to write a report is avoidance.

Watching television or reading a book to 'relax' so that you can work later is a feeble excuse for avoiding work and no real help in getting started. You may feel better indulging in this activity, but it will not help you get the work done.

Learn to correctly label avoidance activities to overcome procrastination.

Jobs that are too big

We often avoid getting to work on a project because it seems to be too big to tackle. Break your task into manageable parts that can be tackled one at a time. Even if you spend a few minutes on each on a regular basis, the task will soon be completed.

For example, planning a presentation can seem a daunting task when you consider the work involved. If your presentation is not imminent, you could ease yourself into it by perhaps starting to work on the objectives or the audience profile, then the Introduction, and so on.

Learn to play

For most of us, learning to play is the most difficult of all objectives. The manager who never has time to take a holiday, or the person so wrapped up in the responsibilities of parenthood that he can never have time to himself, are people who need to learn to take time out for themselves. The pressures of a career and family are dealt with more effectively by people who can get away from them. The person who is not able to play is often irritable and anxious, and very often is not an efficient worker.

By using the methods described here you may be able to find time to play. Many people use play time to 're-ward' themselves after some accomplishment. This kind of self-reinforcement can often help you get more work done.

Changing your behaviour, as well as your thinking, can reduce stress and improve your use of time. The four cornerstones of such an approach are:

- Planning
- Record keeping
- Overcoming procrastination
- Play.

Being more organized in all of these areas can greatly improve your chance of minimizing the stress in your life.

VISUALIZE SUCCESS

'Nothing will ever be attempted if all possible objections must first be overcome.'

Dr. Samuel Johnson

Visualization is being used successfully in areas such as sports training, where coaches are trying to build up the confidence and performance of the athlete.

Firstly think of the event. It could be giving a speech, attending an interview or sitting an exam. Think of the worst thing that could happen. Paint the worst picture you possibly can. What would it be like, for example, if you were to 'dry up'; or if your mind were to go completely blank. By imagining the worst possible scenario, you have acknowledged the fear. Now develop this into a positive outcome. Build up a picture of you giving a wonderful performance and appreciate the warm glow which this produces. In any potentially stressful situation, follow the formula:

Preparation   **Visualization**   **Relaxation**

CONTINGENCY PLANS

Things can and do go wrong occasionally, but with some forethought you can help reduce the possibility. For all business occasions compile a **'What If'** list. Make this part of your preparation. For example, if you are preparing a presentation, at each stage ask yourself what could go wrong. One of your fears might be that the overhead projector may break down. The contingency plan would then be to arrange to have a back-up machine, or carry a spare bulb with you. With good preparation you will reduce the risk of things going wrong. If they do (and sometimes this will be out of your control), you will at least be prepared with a contingency plan.

What If areas to consider for a presentation might include items under the headings of Personal, Material, Equipment, Venue, etc.

Never draw attention to a problem or exacerbate it by dwelling on the matter. Aim for a speedy recovery and continue. Don't tell the audience, for example, 'I seem to have an overhead missing'. Pause – recover the situation – continue.

Self talk for sitting examinations

Everyone at some time in their lives will sit an examination, and most managers are familiar with sitting college, university or professional examinations. Even the event of sitting a driving test is enough to make people break out in a sweat.

Use the visualization technique to deal with this particular type of stress. As in the rest of this book, the first step is **always**:

Preparation

Tell yourself:

'I am doing all I can to prepare – the rest is up to me.'

'I am as bright and knowledgeable as other students who have passed these examinations.'

'I have handled examination situations in the past and have survived.'

'I wouldn't have got this far unless I knew something.'

Finally plan a special treat to celebrate after the event.

3
MEETINGS

'A group that takes minutes and wastes hours'
Milton Berle

Attending and participating in meetings is often cited as a stressful event. Very often this situation is coupled with poor time management and miscommunication. Studies suggest that, in most businesses, between 30 and 55 per cent of committed time is currently being wasted in unproductive meetings.

If properly handled, however, meetings can be productive, and have many key advantages. For example, they help to pool expertise and to tap new sources. They provide up-to-date knowledge of a situation, and can capitalize on the synergy of team working. They also provide an opportunity to encourage participation. Generally, meetings fall into one of three categories:

INFORMATION   DECISION-MAKING   TEAM-BUILDING

Information meetings are held to gather information and share it quickly and accurately to a number of people. This method can avoid message distortion which often happens when information is passed from person to person. An example of this might be when a company is about to communicate redundancies in its three main plants. Meetings can then be planned to take place in these plants for the same date and time, so that management can communicate the message simultaneously to all staff.

Decision-making meetings are held when the person responsible for the decision wants the views of others involved, help in solving a problem, and suggestions for alternative courses of action.

Team-building meetings are held to allow members to get help with their problems, to provide support for members, to encourage members to participate in the affairs of the team, as for example, work groups on quality.

To reduce stress prepare well. The following is a checklist of ideas to help you make future meetings more productive, as Chairperson and as a participant.

GUIDELINES FOR THE CHAIRPERSON

Be punctual
This will help to establish leadership from the start, and enable the Chair to meet and build rapport with the audience. Arriving early is also useful, as preliminary discussions with individuals or on points that might cause difficulty in the meeting itself can be discussed.

Seating
Consider the seating arrangements. Where people sit can affect the feel of a meeting and its efficiency. The Chair who wishes to control this should place name cards to indicate where he would like people to sit.

Timing
Unless there are special circumstances, always start on time. This is professional and courteous to other participants.

Set the tone
In his introductory remarks, the Chair sets the tone for the rest of the meeting. Deal with administration details at this time – catering, finishing time, smoking, etc. Aim to be businesslike but friendly. Keep your objectives in mind.

Matters arising
Keep this short and to the point. This should normally

be a brief reporting on agreed actions that have (or have not) been taken since the previous meeting.

Visual aids

Visual aids can be a great help in controlling a meeting. For example, in a fairly small group of around 20 people, a flip chart is a useful aid. Points can be noted on a blank flip chart. It is an aide memoire and also forms the basis of the subsequent record.

DISCUSSION

For managers new to the skills of chairmanship, the discussion stage of the meeting is often viewed with trepidation. One of the key problems is deciding when to press for the final decision. Clearly, timing is important.

Shaping the discussion

Introduction

The aim of this phase is to gain attention and focus in on the subject at issue. In formal meetings, each item of business will be in the form of a motion introduced by a proposer. In less formal meetings, it is helpful for each item to be introduced by a subject leader.

Delineation

This is the stage where participants state the issues to be decided.

Debate

Alliances are made at this stage, and differences clarified. Opinions are formed and firmed up. The Chair should keep his own views hidden at least until the discussion is well under way. Typically one speaker makes a suggestion, a second disagrees, and others then line up behind the two points of view, leading to a lengthy, and possibly heated, debate. Often, less forceful participants may hold back from speaking out. The flip chart method is useful here, if the Chair calls for ideas which are then written on the flip chart; before allowing criticism, there is a greater chance that everyone will have their say.

Decision

This is the most difficult part of the discussion session. The Chair will need to spot the point at which it is right to press for a decision. To reach this point too quickly or too late may result in discontented participants and poor decision making.

Universal consensus is the ideal method of decision making. The Chair must decide when this can be achieved. Again the flip chart can prove useful here. Often there is doubt or confusion as to what decision is being suggested. A form of words written down on the flip chart provides a focus as the point of decision is approached.

Alternatives to consensus

For a variety of reasons consensus may not be possible, and the following possible solutions will need to be considered.

Imposed decision

The Chair, having listened to the discussion, can impose an arbitrary decision. This makes sense if he is someone who holds authority over the group, for example the manager of a department.

Subcommittee

A working party may be set up, to report back to a later meeting.

Adjournment

The discussion can be adjourned to give people time to think further, do more research or consult colleagues.

Vote

A vote can be taken. This can be simply a show of hands. If the subject is delicate and individuals may be compromised by the above method, a secret ballot might be considered.

Control

More meetings are damaged by poor chairmanship than by clear direction. By using the flip chart method of recording ideas, there is a greater chance that everyone's ideas will be heard. This means that some can be ruled out right away, and others will be seen as worth consideration. Balanced debate can then commence on the remainder.

When a productive meeting ends, the members go away with a feeling of achievement and improve morale. To ensure that future meetings are productive, use the following checklist.

PRODUCTIVE MEETINGS CHECKLIST

1. Call a meeting only if absolutely necessary. Consider other forms of communication.
2. Clearly define the meeting objectives. Are they SMART?
3. Choose the members of the meeting carefully. Ask, 'What can they contribute?'
4. Choose a suitable venue and time to suit the majority of members.
5. Advise members, well in advance of the meeting, of the objectives, agenda, time and place, so that they can do some preparation.
6. Plan your strategy for the meeting. Consider any potential problems, for example strong personalities who may need special handling. Prepare yourself and your material.
7. Ensure that there will be no interruptions. Check

the meeting room, equipment, room layout and catering arrangements.

8. Call the meeting to order as soon as possible, welcome the members and state the objectives briefly.
9. Ask open-ended questions
10. Keep control, stimulate discussion but keep members' contributions short and to the point.
11. Summarize the important points raised.
12. Bring the meeting to a timely close and thank members for their contribution. Record agreement and action decided and circulate these to members.

If you are a *member* of a meeting the following is a list of key points to make your attendance more productive and enjoyable.

Helping Meetings Work

- Make sure you know the objectives of the meeting and what is expected of you
- Know your own objectives for attending. What result do you want at the end of the day?
- Find out how long the meeting is planned to last. Block this time out of your schedule and make only that amount of time available. Arrive on time and fully prepared
- Keep contributions short and to the point
- When the agenda has been completed stand up and ask to be excused (If the meeting does not finish in the allotted time point this out to the Chair and ask how much longer you will be required to attend as you have other matters to see to.)
- Ensure that you receive a copy of the minutes. Take prompt action on anything affecting you.

4

SPEAKING IN PUBLIC

'My husband will read my speech.'
Queen Elizabeth to the Duke of Edinburgh, as she stood up to speak at the Opening of Parliament and discovered she had forgotten her spectacles.

If you find speaking in public particularly stressful, keep in mind that most people hold this view, even those who do it for a living. Many professional actors recommend the following methods to reduce nerves. It also helps generate energy, and reduces negative feelings like anger, anxiety, depression and fatigue.

- Sit in a straight–backed chair. Carry your rib cage high, but not in a ramrod–straight military position. Incline slightly forward
- Now put your hands together just in front of your chest, your elbows akimbo, your fingertips pointing upwards, and push so that you feel an isometric opposing force in the heels of your palms and under your arms
- Say 'ssss', like a hiss. As you exhale the sound, contract the muscles in the vital triangle as though you are rowing a boat against a current, pulling the oars back. The vital triangle should feel like a tightening corset
- Relax the muscles at the end of your exhalation, then inhale again.

Contracting those muscles prevents the production of noradrenaline and epinephrine, the fear-producing chemicals in your system. So, when you want to shake off nervousness, sit with your vital triangle contracted, your lips slightly parted and release your breath over your lower teeth on a slight hiss. You can do this any-where. (There are further relaxation exercises later in the book.)

Someone once said that a well-prepared speech is already nine-tenths delivered. There is some truth in this. The following list will help to assess if you have in-cluded the key elements required for a well-prepared speech.

PREPARATION CHECKLIST

- Title of Preparation
- What is my aim/objective(s)
- What results do I want?
- Who are my Audience?
- What is their background?
- How many will there be?
- What are their needs?
- How long have I got?
- What are the main points I want to get across? (Do I have a logical structure?)
- What are their main objections/questions?
- How will I open? Drama/Curiosity/Story/By ask-ing a question?
- What is the hook? (i.e. what's in it for them?)
- How will I build rapport?
- How will I close?
- How will I add interest? Analogies/Example/Story/Opinion?
- What other hardware?
    Flipchart
    Overhead projector

Lets look briefly at the above headings.

Objectives
This is a good preparation starting point. What is the

purpose of the talk? Are you trying to inform, motivate, persuade? Keep your objective short and simple. For example it may be 'to inform employees of the new benefits package', or 'to motivate staff to improve customer service'.

Audience
Spend some time researching your audience. The more you know about them, the better you can tailor your talk to their needs. Who are they, who do they represent, etc? Most importantly, why are they listening to you, and what will make them sit up and listen to what you have to say?

Structuring the talk
Check that you have a sound structure. Quite simply, this means a beginning, a middle and an end.

Follow the three-part structure
The Opening and Introduction – The Body – The Close. This is often summarized as:

- Tell them what you are going to tell them – The Opening
- Tell them – The Body, including the key points
- Tell them what you have told them – The Close

It's a tried and tested formula that works.

Aim to spend about 75 per cent of the total time available in the Body section with 10 per cent in the Introduction and 15 per cent in the Close.

THE OPENING
It is essential to hook the audience attention from the minute you take the stage. To make a good first impression:

- Stand and face the audience

- Pause, and smile, providing it is not a serious topic.
- Hook their attention in your first few words
- Choose the opening that is appropriate for the audience and presentation objectives.

Introduction

Tell them your name and, if relevant, your job title, company, and a little background information about yourself. This helps establish credibility. Usually the presenter has been asked to give the presentation because he is the person who has expertise in the subject to be presented. This should be brief, and should raise the comfort level of the audience, i.e. here is someone who sounds knowledgeable.

Subject

Give them the title of your talk and make it provocative. The title acts as a stimulus; it should play to your purpose and ideally, your point.

Give your audience clear signposts. Tell them where you intend to take them within your subject. Signposting establishes several important factors. It shows that you know where you are going, and that there is a logical progression within your talk; and it also defines the limits within which you will work.

Tell them how long the presentation will last.

Other

Set the ground rules for questions. Decide if you will take them during the presentation or afterwards and inform the audience. You will be more in control of timing if you take questions at the end. However, it is often beneficial to invite questions throughout the presentation, particularly if the subject matter involves detailed or technical information.

Tell the audience if you have materials to give them.

Only give them out at this point if they need to refer to them during the presentation.

THE BODY

You have now introduced yourself and your subject to the audience.

The Body is the section where you will put across your information, arguments, key points on the subject. It should resemble a route map, with frequent signposting leading your audience towards your objectives. The key skill in this section is to maintain audience interest and attention. Use some of the following to do this:

- Make use of examples, anecdotes, statistics, quotations. Keep these meaningful and relevant to the subject and audience
- Use humour. Check that your jokes are in good taste. An original joke is best. The safest joke is the one against yourself. Humorous stories are a valuable addition to most presentations, as long as they observe the above rules
- Support material. This can make the simplest, most ordinary subject come alive. Visual aids will help you connect and link ideas together. They are also useful for maintaining audience interest.

How you present the information will have a bearing on attention levels. When presenting information, present the **major idea** – detail – detail – **Recap**.

For **bad news**, or to **persuade**: **Hint** – detail – detail – detail – **Major Idea** – **Recap**.

To present ideas to management, use this simple mnemonic: Preface, Position, Problem, Possibility, Proposal, Postscript.

Limitations

If what you propose has a limitation, present it in the

first half of your sentence, and then present the benefits which will trade that off. **Always** put the limitation first.

THE CLOSE

Many presenters start working on the Close of the presentation before any other area, and work backwards. Endings should be bold and brief.

Types of close

- Ask the audience to take some specific action
- Outline alternative actions for the audience
- Express confidence in what the audience will do about the matter
- Express confidence that the problem will be resolved.

Other endings

- Use a suitable quotation from someone known to the audience, or from literature
- Use an illustration
- End with a humorous story.

The close is the last chance to reprise your main points, so recap these briefly. Draw any conclusions and ask for action if this is appropriate.

You may wish to thank the audience, and should always end on a positive note.

Note: The three-part structure given in this section can be used for all the management situations featured in this book. Using a structure gives the topic a 'shape'. This means that you have a skeleton on which to build your information.

Checklist of the five key elements of audience interest and recall.

Power

- Begin powerfully. Everything about you should come across as being positive, including your stance and your voice
- Let your enthusiasm show. Let the audience see how happy you are to be talking to them
- Communicate with your audience – don't lecture them. Involve them as soon as possible.

Repeat

Your audience will be better able to remember points that you repeat regularly. It could be a phrase or a saying. Commercial advertisers use this technique. Count the number of times the product name or telephone number is repeated in a short space of time.

Emphasize

Stimulate your audience; present your facts in a variety of ways which will help them remember your key points.

Maximize involvement

Ask rhetorical questions to increase audience interest and attention.

End on a high

Make your ending unforgettable!

CONTROLLING NERVES

'What makes a professional is that you are used to being afraid. You accept fear.'

The following ideas may help with controlling nerves:

- Prepare thoroughly – Remember 90 per cent Preparation, 10 per cent Perspiration

- Pay particular attention of your Opening – Learn it by heart and put feeling into it. A successful Opening will make you feel less nervous, and forms the basis on which to build the rest of the talk
- Build in audience participation – this takes the heat off you
- Adopt a pleasant attitude – your audience will want you to succeed
- Use positive language, avoid jargon and clichés
- Be enthusiastic and friendly – it will rub off on the audience
- If you feel that your throat may dry up, have some water near to hand, but not on the table or lectern (in case of accident)
- Always stand to talk; it adds gravitas. If you are conscious of shaking, a lectern may help. This is particularly useful when speaking to a large group
- Avoid alcohol, coffee and other stimulants if possible. If you must, have enough only to relax you
- Make sure you are comfortable with your surroundings and equipment. A thorough rehearsal before the event helps reduce nerves
- Try to relax before giving the talk. Some people find deep breathing exercises helpful.

Remember: Fear is a normal experience, whether you are speaking up at a meeting, attending an interview, sitting an exam.

- The fact that you are nervous indicates that you are like other people
- Fears are generally not well founded: speakers do not die, or even faint, while delivering a talk
- Nervousness tends to reduce with experience
- Speakers seldom look as frightened as they feel. People rarely see the speaker's knees tremble or hands shake.

If you are **well prepared you almost always give creditable performances**.

Pitfalls for the Nervous

'The quickest route to fluency is Macon Blanc.'

It is very difficult for speakers to resist the temptation to have a drink before delivering their speech, particularly on after-dinner, business, and celebratory occasions, where good food and wine are part of the enjoyment of the event. Beware! Dutch courage can do more harm than good.

If your throat is dry, stick to mineral water. Sip water during pauses in your speech. If you sip alcohol while you speak, you will give the impression of being desperate. If you feel it will help, try to stick to one drink before you rise. One drink may stimulate and relax you; any more, and your thought processes will slow down, speech may become slurred and your reflexes will be clumsy. Try to eat a minimum of food, however delicious. Too much food could also slow you down, or give you indigestion.

If you are delivering your speech from behind a table or lectern, common for business speeches, you may find a jug of water placed before you on the table. Before you start your speech, move the water (or coffee, etc.) away from the table. I have witnessed many speeches which have been literally a washout. It is difficult to recover credibility if you accidentally spill liquid over your notes or overheads.

Finally, when applause greets your final words and you sit down, you will experience a rush of adrenalin. You have acquitted yourself well, and are relieved it's all over. Watch out for signs of over excitability. That knotted stomach may have prevented you from eating earlier, but now you want to eat and drink everything in sight. Remember you want to live to perform again!

5

THE RECRUITMENT INTERVIEW

> 'This woman is headstrong, obstinate and dangerously self-opinionated.'
>
> Report by Personnel Officer, ICI, 1948
> (Rejecting Margaret Thatcher for a job)

There are many types of interview; each for a specific purpose. For example, recruitment, appraisal, coaching, disciplinary. Interview situations can be stressful for both interviewer and interviewee. It is a particularly artificial situation, and therefore building up a rapport between yourself and the interviewee is essential. Rapport is established when both sides communicate clearly, freely, openly and with due seriousness. It evolves from an understanding between you that you are conducting the interview because the interviewer is trying to collect information given by the interviewee, and making decisions on this.

MANAGING THE INTERVIEW

There are several areas to consider in planning and conducting an interview. Many of these will be relevant to many different types of interviews. The following is a list of topics which you will need to address during the preparation stage.

1. Building rapport – warming up
2. Controlling the interview
3. Questioning
4. Listening skills
5. Problem areas

INTRODUCTION

Warming up

Establishing rapport is an essential element of a good interview. Here are some hints:

- Before the interview take time to read through the interviewee's application form, CV and other information about them
- Outline your objectives
- Make a note of particular aspects you wish to bring up at the interview. Formulate questions in the light of the job description and interviewee experience
- Check the interview venue. If relevant, check that the interview room has been booked, laid out correctly, refreshments and any administrative details taken care of
- Ensure that the interview room is as comfortable and as pleasant as possible
- If possible, personally greet the interviewee as he arrives. Introduce yourself and show him to the interview room
- Briefly outline the purpose of the interview and the areas you intend to cover.

Look at this warming up period as a time to set the guidelines for the interview, and also to put the interviewee at ease. By telling them at the start of the interview the broad areas you are going to cover and the order in which you will do so, you will give them a sense of purpose and direction. (This is where your preparation work will prove useful.)

Example of a simple introductory overview:

Interviewer: 'Thank you for sending me your application form. We'll be looking at each of the areas covered in more detail, starting with your present job, then previous work experience.

Then I would like to ask you some questions about your professional qualifications. Finally you'll have a chance to ask me any questions about the job or the company.

Okay? Then let's begin with . . .'

(If the applicant is a school-leaver or graduate, you could start by asking about their education.)

Controlling the interview
Control in this case doesn't mean forcing the interview to go the way you want it to go. Rather, you are directing and guiding the interviewee, by giving them the space and freedom to express themselves. Controlling also means knowing how to motivate the applicant to speak out, as well as knowing how to stop the interviewee who has difficulty knowing when to stop.

QUESTIONING TECHNIQUE

Objectives
A good question is one that encourages the interviewee to answer freely and honestly. A bad question is one that inhibits the interviewee from answering freely or produces distorted information. The questions you ask and the method you use should:

1. Obtain the information you require.
2. Motivate the interviewee to talk freely.

To achieve this, your questions should be:

- Short and to the point
- Asked one at a time
- Unambiguous
- Phrased positively
- Restricted to the subject matter of the interview.

Type of Question	Objective	Likely outcome in terms of type of information collected	Examples
1. Open-ended?	To establish rapport at start of conversation	Facts, opinions	How are things? How was the traffic this morning?
	To open up a particular topic	Facts, opinions, suggestions	What ideas do you have about . . . ?
	To discover the interviewee's feelings	Opinions	How do you feel about . . . ? What's your attitude towards . . . ?
2. Closed?	To collect specific pieces of information	Facts	How long have you worked for the company? What time did you arrive?
	To gain confirmation or otherwise of precise information	Facts, opinions in yes or no form	Do you agree? Is your title 'Sales Manager'?
3. Follow-up	To show interest and encourage person to continue talking	More facts, opinions and suggestions	Ah? So? And then?
	To increase the quantity and/or quality of information collected so far	More facts, opinions and suggestions and/or more perceptive insightful comments	What evidence have you? Can you tell me some more about what happened? How do you mean? Why do you say that?

Type of Question	Objective	Likely outcome in terms of type of information collected	Examples
3. Follow-up contd.	To confirm your own understanding of information collected so far	Clearer restatement of earlier facts, opinions and suggestions	So how we see it is as follows? If I've heard correctly what you are saying is?

Write down the questions that must be answered:

- Don't trust to memory, particularly if you are an inexperienced interviewer
- Place your list in a convenient place where you can glance at it without disturbing the interviewee
- Use a highlighter pen (as recommended for presentation notes). This means that you can quickly glance at the key word and then concentrate on giving attention to the applicant.

Questions to avoid
- leading questions
- trick questions
- jargon-loaded questions
- impertinent questions.

Phrase questions positively
If you want the interviewee to answer positively and with confidence you too must convey an air of confidence. Speak with conviction, for example:

'Could you tell me . . .', rather than the apologetic approach, 'I wonder if you could perhaps tell me . . .'

Focus attention on the particular areas you wish to expand. Don't ask vague questions, for example:

'Could you tell me a little about yourself?'

This is too vague and unspecific, and invites the response 'what do you want to know?' Unfocused questions like this give the impression that you have not prepared yourself thoroughly.

Look at the application form and find areas which perhaps need some clarification. For example:

Interviewer: 'You say in your application form that in your last job you did not feel you received the promotion you deserved. Why do you think this was the case?'

Move from the general to the specific. Outline the general area of your interest, and then follow this up with specific questions.

Ask open questions to receive open replies. The five Ws will help you do this: Who, Where, When, What and Why. You could also add How.

LISTENING SKILLS

As well as developing good questioning technique, the interviewer should also practise good listening skills. Remember you are trying to build bridges with your interviewees, not barriers.

Barriers to good listening

On-off listening

This unfortunate habit in listening arises from the fact that most of us think about four times as fast as the average person speaks. Thus the listener has three-quarters of a minute of spare thinking time for each listening minute. Sometimes we use this extra time to think of our own personal affairs, concerns or interests instead of listening.

Concentrate on the responses you receive to your questions.

Open ears – closed mind listening
Sometimes we decide rather quickly, particularly after a long day of interviews, that the interviewee is unsuitable or their answers predictable. We shut off.

Subject centred instead of speaker centred
Often we concentrate on the problem and not the person. Detail and fact about an incident become more important than what people are saying about themselves.

Fact listening
We listen to people and try to remember the facts. As we do this, frequently the speaker has gone on to new facts and we lose them in the process.

Red-flag listening
To some of us certain words are like a red flag to a bull. When we hear them, we get upset or irritated and stop listening.

Interrupting
Question time in parliament is a good example of this problem. Constant interruptions do not allow the other speaker to speak freely. Background hubbub, noise or movement of people does not help.

Good listening skills
There are a number of aids to effective listening:

- Active listening involves the use of appropriate gestures and noises of encouragement such as smiles, nods and grunts. Words interjected at the right moment will have the same effect: 'Yes', 'I see', etc.
- It is important to give the person talking good eye contact. Avoid distracting actions such as glancing out of the window or looking at your watch
- Avoid preconceptions. If we think we know what

the speaker is about to say, not only do we fail to listen, but we may be convinced we have heard something that was not said.

Body language

The body language of the interviewer and interviewee can aid the listening process. The interviewer can use body language to stimulate a response, by leaning forward and using positive facial expressions. By observing the body language of the interviewee, the interviewer can build upon his understanding of the responses. Small movements of the hands, narrowing or opening of the eyes, eye contact or lack of it and facial expression may suggest tension, doubt, disagreement.

Between the lines

Hearing between the lines is a bit like reading a CV. What is **not** said can be more important than what **is** said. Interviewees will naturally play down or ignore aspects of any possible answer they think may be unfavourable to them, while making much of those aspects they believe to be favourable. The effective interviewer will look out for this behaviour. For example:

Interviewer: 'Was your marketing proposal implemented?'

Interviewee: 'My proposal was very well received. The Managing Director himself congratulated me, and the Sales Manager said my idea was brilliant.'

Interviewer: 'Was it implemented?'

Interviewee: 'No.'

Politicians are adept at avoiding answering directly.

Mrs Thatcher herself was an expert. On an official visit to Edinburgh during Chancellor Lawson's budget, she was asked, 'Prime Minister, what do you think of Nigel Lawson's budget?' Her reply: 'Edinburgh is a flourishing city!'

Summary and restatement by the interviewer of what he believes the interviewee has said is a useful check that he has understood. For example:

'So, if I hear you correctly, you feel that the period you spent on the Graduate Training Scheme was of value in your personal development, but felt towards the end of your training that there was no challenging job awaiting you?'

Evaluation
This involves judging the credibility and completeness of the reply, the interviewee's motivation in giving it, and its bearing on the other aspects of what you need to know. Replies need to be compared during the course of the interview to ensure consistency. For example:

'I'm sorry, but if I heard you correctly earlier, you were saying that you were totally responsible for the marketing budget. What you have just said suggests to me that this needed sign–off from someone else. Can you enlighten me on this?'

Be aware of the **halo effect**, or the tendency to judge what the interviewee has said later in the light of earlier favourable or unfavourable replies.

For example, an interviewee may have a PhD, or an excellent career record with a prestigious company. Our satisfaction at these may prevent us from giving full weight to his unsatisfactory job performance.

Ending the interview
The objectives of this part of the interview are to:

- Answer interviewee's questions
- Give them a chance to add anything to what has already been said
- Explain what will happen next.

Answering interviewee's questions

The interviewee will come along for interview with questions which he would like answered. Many of these will be answered during the interview, but it is important to schedule in some time at the end for final questions. For example, the interviewer might say:

'Are there any aspects of the job you are still not clear about, or any other questions you would like to ask?'

The kind of question asked can often give us further information about the candidate, and the areas which he considered important. For example:

'Yes, I would like to study for a professional degree at night class. Will the company pay the fees?'

This part of the interview is also important for the interviewee to correct any wrong impressions he may have given, perhaps as a result of nervousness. You might end an interview by asking:

'Is there anything we haven't given you the chance to say?'

Finally – next steps

The interviewee should be clear what will happen next, and when it is likely to happen. For example:

'Well, thank you for all the information you have given me. I need now to go away and digest this. I expect to make a decision by Friday, so you will hear from me next week. I hope you won't mind if I contact you again if I discover anything else I need to know.'

In selection interviews it is important to say nothing that could be interpreted as a comment on how the interview has gone or the view you have formed of the candidate. Comments such as 'I'll see you again' can be misinterpreted.

If the interview has achieved its objectives, there will be several important tasks to complete afterwards. These are likely to include:

- Writing up results
- Final evaluation
- Action.

Insufficient time spent in defining the candidate evaluation criteria is often a cause of stress for the interviewer. Criteria can be defined as 'musts' – no candidate can be considered further unless he meets them. (Remember these must be measurable.) The remainder criteria will be 'wants', and can be scored.

The evaluation process, whether by an individual or group, should be completed by asking the question: 'If we choose this candidate, **what might go wrong**?' By asking this question, unexplored factors and unexplained doubts can emerge. This may lead to obtaining further information or references.

Recruitment interview Checklist

1. Read all paperwork well in advance.
2. Prepare questions from the information you have on the candidate. (Match these to the job description.)
3. Prepare an evaluation checklist of 'musts' and 'wants'.
4. Check interview administration, room, time etc.
5. Welcome the candidate warmly and be aware of your body language – keep it positive.

6. Explain the procedure.
7. Ask open questions and listen to the answers.
8. Probe gaps and unsatisfactory replies throughout.
9. Give interviewee ample opportunity to ask questions.
10. Conclude the interview on a positive note and inform the candidate of what the next steps are.

BODY LANGUAGE

One-to-one interview
Be aware of your body language in one-to-one interview situations, such as appraisal, information exchanges, meeting clients, etc.

- Sit as close as appropriate. A 90°-120° orientation will reduce the threat of appearing dominant or over friendly
- Turn at least head and shoulders directly to client
- Lean towards client
- Legs crossed at start, uncross them as you become comfortable
- Hands loosely held in lap
- Tilt head when listening
- Take notes
- 'Match' their body language as appropriate.

What to look for
(This also applies to group presentation.)

Think of people like flowers: closed and they are defensive, negative; open and they are warm, receptive. Head down = negative. Head up = interested. Head to the side, perhaps with a finger vertical up to the cheekbone = evaluating, deeply interested.

If you are slow, boring or covering known ground, the audience gets impatient, tapping, twitching, and fiddling with things.

If they have had enough, they turn to something else, such as a diary or another paper. They look at their watch or the clock; they even look longingly at the door!

If they are bored, they become lethargic, stop looking at you and put their heads down or in their hands, eyes half-shut.

People move all the time. Look for feedback, and match how you work to how they react. Unless you must stick to a script, be driven by the audience, not by your notes. If the audience turns off, you waste your time and theirs.

SEATING ARRANGEMENTS

The seating arrangement is one of the first things a person sees on entering the room. It should give a message that says: 'I am approachable and I am interested in what you have to say.' The seating arrangement should not say 'I am more important than you.'

In an interview situation you could perhaps sit at right angles to each other at a table, or sit facing each other with nothing between you. If you need something to put notes on, a small side table placed to the side will help. Placing a table or desk between you and the interviewee creates a barrier.

Even in the most difficult interviews, such as those involving discipline or dismissal, you and the interviewee are on the same side, and therefore there should be no reason to separate the two of you.

The same applies to presentations. Unless there is not a choice, for example you must use a full lectern with fixed microphone, try and stand in front of the table instead of behind.

That table or desk also represents a psychological barrier to good communication. You may be surprised to know that you will feel **less** stressed if you dispose of it. Whether you are communicating with one person in an interview, ten in a meeting, or fifty in an audience, aim for a communication style that is similar to having a one-to-one conversation.

The interviewee should feel that all of your attention is concentrated on him, and in a large group, members of the audience should feel the same.

Let the natural feelings in your body come out. Use your gestures and movements to add a dimension to your words.

Always stand to make a speed or presentation. Get close to the audience if you can. Staying away suggests you are frightened. Come down from your position; reach out and get them to join with you.

Hold yourself well. Make sure your stance is balanced. Never twist, slump or lean. Look out and speak out. Hold your head up and project your voice to the back of the room.

The following are some ideas for room/seating layout. Choose which style is appropriate for the size, degree of participation and formality of the meeting.

Common arrangements include:

- Horseshoe
- Boardroom
- Herring-bone
- Round table
- Theatre-style
- Negotiating

- Schoolroom
- Freestyle

Members of small, participative meetings will usually be seated round one large table in a boardroom or other meeting room. If, however, there is to be a presentation, it may be better use the horseshoe (u-shape) with a table with overhead or slide projector at the open end. This is also a suitable arrangement for training, the main advantage being that the trainer or presenter can actually 'walk into' his audience.

For large meetings, the choice is between theatre and schoolroom. The only difference being that the schoolroom has tables. This is best if there are handouts, and the audience are likely to take notes, or if the room would look empty with just the seating.

Theatre-style is often favoured when there is a large audience, with guest speakers usually sitting at the front facing the audience.

6

ATTENDING A SELECTION INTERVIEW

Many people find this one of the most stressful situations to be in. Today more is at stake when applying for jobs, as competition is fierce, and employers can take their pick from well qualified candidates.

PLANNING

Only ten per cent of people get jobs through newspaper ads. More and more employers are cutting costs by relying on word of mouth to find suitable candidates. Here are some tips on finding a job in this way:

- Contact ex-colleagues if you intend returning to the same type of work
- Cold call people in your target profession for an informal discussion. Prepare questions to elicit information. They may be able to suggest other people to talk to
- Tell everyone – ex-colleagues, friends, family – that you are job-hunting
- Read books and relevant trade journals to find out which companies are expanding etc.

It is essential that you prepare a professional CV. This may be the first contact you have with a company. First impressions count. The following are some general guidelines for compiling your CV. When you have completed the final version, you can amend for future use, leaving out or adding details as appropriate.

CHECKLIST FOR A PROFESSIONAL CV

1. Use quality white paper.
2. Simple layout, avoid folders.

3. Set out neatly using word-processor or typewriter. (Many companies now offer a CV service.)
4. Make your sentences short. Begin with a verb, and keep language positive. For example, **Conducted** training programmes, **Developed** marketing strategy, **Compiled** procedure manual, **Interviewed** graduates.
5. Concentrate on skills relevant to the job description. Only include interests which demonstrate a skill, eg. learning a language.
6. Unless you have recently graduated, don't give too much information on education.
7. Check your CV thoroughly, ask someone else to look at it and make comments.
8. Check your career history for gaps. An employer may ask about this. An example might be that you have a six-month gap when you were unemployed. Think about this in positive terms, for example, you may have learned word processing during this time to enable you to produce more professional CVs or attended classes to further your education.
9. The chronological type of CV is the traditional format. List your career history starting with current or last job and work backwards.
   - State each job title
   - Company name and address
   - Period of employment with dates
   - Job description
   - Special achievements, awards etc.
   - Educational qualifications – working back.

PLANNING TO REDUCE STRESS

When you finally discover that you have been selected for interview, the initial feeling of elation is often replaced by a whole series of stressful doubts, such as:

- How many others are on the short list?
- How many of them are better qualified than me?

- What is the interviewer going to be like?
- Will there be more than one interviewer?

Although interviews can be nerve-racking, interviewers are not out to ask you trick questions. They are simply trying to match your skills and personality to the job. Planning is essential if you want to show yourself in a positive light.

INTERVIEW CHECKLIST

Before the interview

- Obtain an up-to-date job description for the post that you are applying for
- Outline all the qualities and skills required for the position and think of how you can match them and prove you are suited
- Try and anticipate questions you are likely to be asked. Some standard questions may include:
  - Why you want the job
  - Why you are leaving your present employment
  - Your strongest/weakest points
- Ask personnel to send relevant information on the company. Check the library or Chamber of Commerce for any additional information you require.

From this information, draw up two or three questions which will show the interviewer that you are interested in the company, for example, 'I read recently in *Marketing Update* that . . .'

- Practise the interview with a friend
- Make up a 'You' list of five or six positive items about yourself. This will satisfy the question: 'Tell me about yourself'
- Decide on an acceptable financial package – but let the interviewer raise it.

Personal preparation

- Remember, first impressions count. Prepare your clothes the evening before. As a general rule, aim to be smart and professional
- Do what you can to make yourself feel good inside, you'll present yourself well on the outside
- If you are not sure about how to get to the interview, call the company and ask for directions. Work out how you will get there
- Aim to arrive with time to spare.

On the day

- Read a newspaper on the morning of the interview, as you may be asked questions on topical issues
- If you have surplus bags, dripping umbrella or overcoat, leave these at reception
- Check with reception the name of the interviewer (This may have changed.)
- Look around; could you work in these conditions? Do people seem comfortable talking to each other? What is your impression of the culture? Do they use first names, etc?

The interview

- Smile and shake hands firmly
- Wait to be invited to sit down. If the wait seems too long ask, 'Where would you like me to sit?'
- Aim to feel relaxed when you sit down to be interviewed. You will probably feel nervous, but try to give the impression of confidence
- Avoid negative body language
- Address the interviewer by name, particularly at first
- Lean forward slightly towards the interviewer (shows interest) and don't slouch

- Give the interviewer good eye contact
- Sit comfortably with arms and legs uncrossed
- Don't fiddle with hair, jewellery, tie, cufflinks
- Never smoke
- Be positive about your good points and play down your weak ones. Always be honest
- If you do not understand a question, ask for clarification, don't try and fudge
- Before you leave the interview ask when you can expect to get feedback.

After the interview

- Jot down your reactions. For example, were there any unexpected or difficult questions? This will give you an opportunity to brush up these for next time
- Write to the interviewer the day following your interview, thanking them for seeing you. This is also an ideal opportunity to add any further relevant information you have have overlooked. Keep this letter short and to the point
- If you do not hear from the company within the stated time, contact them. Don't hassle them and don't complain. Let them know if you have been offered another job
- If you have been put forward by a recruitment agency call them, as soon as you can, to let them know how you got on and to confirm your interest in the job. They will almost certainly feed this straight back to the interviewer and it will be viewed positively
- If at the end of the day you don't get the job, put it down to experience. If you feel that you didn't present yourself in your best light, then resolve to be better prepared next time.

Common interview questions

- Why did you leave?

- What makes a good employer?
- What did you enjoy doing at . . .?
- What are your greatest strengths and weaknesses?
- How would you describes your career progress to date?
- Why did you become (job title)?
- What area of work do you feel least confident about?
- What have been your best achievements?
- What do you know about our company?
- Why do you want this job?
- How do you relax?
- What have you been doing since you left . . . ?
- Why do you want this job?
- Are you being interviewed for any other jobs? Which do you want?

7

THE DISCIPLINARY INTERVIEW

A recent survey shows that over 90 per cent of managers viewed this type of interview as being the number one stressor, along with giving bad news, eg. redundancy notice.

Some of the key fears include:

- Fear of saying the wrong thing
- Feeling uncomfortable, particularly if the manager is not a disciplinarian
- Distaste of the after effect, i.e. unpleasant atmosphere
- Apprehension on the part of the manager that he looks nervous
- Inability to choose appropriate words and phrases
- Clash of strong personalities.

FIVE POINT PLAN TO REDUCE STRESS

Follow this five point plan to help reduce stress:

1. Facts

Double check all the facts. Make sure that you have access to **all** the information before embarking on a reprimand.

2. Act natural

There is no need to put on an 'act'. Be serious, but be yourself.

3. Be fair

Having arrived at the well-considered decision that a reprimand is necessary, get to the point. Avoid giving a lecture. Most important of all **never**, by word, mood or gesture indicate that you bear a grudge.

4. Keep calm

Aim to stay in control. Although you may be tempted, never lose your temper. This will only give you more stress.

5. Be brief

Wording the reprimand is often a cause for concern. Aim to make it succinct and brief. The subject will be well aware of the extent of the transgression, so there is little point in sustaining the action. Suit the words to the personality of the subject. Quite simply, that which constitutes a devastating dress-down in one person's eyes will be water off a duck's back so far as another is concerned.

Once the disciplinary occasion is over, it's over.

8

THE APPRAISAL INTERVIEW

Most companies have some form of appraisal system, and this can be a stressful event for the manager. Having completed his nail-biting writing of the employee report, he now faces the prospect of the face-to-face interview. His stress will be heightened if he:

- believes he is a poor interviewer
- has had no training
- has no faith in the appraisal system
- has had bad experiences of these interviews in the past.

If you lack faith in the appraisal system adopted by your company, ask yourself if your attitude is well-founded, or does it arise from pure bias or prejudice? The continued use of a poor appraisal scheme is not only absurd, but also highly damaging to working relationships and morale.

If it is simply a matter of lack of training, then there are many courses available to help, or you might ask an experienced colleague to give you some coaching.

There are many different types of appraisal interview, and timescales, the most common being the yearly assessment. The purpose of the interview is to exchange information with the employee, discuss performance to date, and also to plan for the future.

To be effective, the appraisal should be based on performance. This means measuring against SMART objectives (see page 24), which the employee should have in writing. The following is a general checklist to help you formulate your approach. Items can be added or deleted as appropriate.

PREPARATION

- Agree a time and place with the interviewee for the appraisal. Give him plenty notice of this so that he can prepare thoroughly
- Ask beforehand if there is anything he would specifically like to discuss. This will alert you as to any special preparation needed
- Plan the interview as a two-way conversation
- Allow time for you and the employee to speak for as long as is necessary to come to an agreement
- Check that you have a quiet room for the interview, and make sure that you have no interruptions
- Ensure that you have a copy of the employee objectives for the job
- Gather information on employee performance from appropriate sources. For example, colleagues who work with him, clients, customers
- If your company appraisal policy involves filling in an appraisal form, then either make notes in pencil on the form, or make separate notes before you go into the interview
- Work out how you will conduct the interview. For example, you may systematically work through the appraisal form. Prepare specific questions.

THE INTERVIEW

- Begin by stating the purpose of the interview, and outline how you intend to proceed. This is a potentially stressful situation for both manager and employee, so it is important to set the scene
- Start by asking a general question, for example, 'Tell me how you feel the job is going.' This will help break the ice, and also may indicate the employee's areas of concern
- Proceed through the appraisal form, discussing each section in detail

- Ask for employee's input on each section before you put your views across
- When you and the employee are in agreement about performance, jot down main discussion points on the form (in pencil)
- Remember this is an opportunity to look forward as well as back. Encourage the employee to talk about his career goals
- Agree new objectives and performance standards with employee
- Following the interview, expand on your notes, and complete the form in pen, or have it typed up
- Give the employee an opportunity to look at the form in detail before he signs it. Perhaps he would like to take it home.

(Information gathering should be completed **before** the interview. For example, speaking to the interviewee's colleagues, customers, and others who liaise with him.)

For the employee

Prepare for your appraisal. If you prepare well for this interview, you will feel less stressed. Be prepared to do at least as much talking as your manager.

- Gather all relevant information
- Read the appraisal form
- Make your own notes to take with you to the interview
- Make an assessment of your performance standard for each section
- Be prepared to back up your assessment.

Hint: Keep a record of your work. Make a note of any tasks which are not in your objectives, but which you have undertaken, for example, taking on extra responsibilities when staff are off sick. File letters of thanks or congratulations for a job well done, from clients, and customers.

Appraisal should not be the only time when manager and employee communicate. Ideally they should meet regularly to assess objectives, and adjust if necessary. By communicating they will fulfil the golden rule of performance appraisal:

NO SURPRISES

DELEGATION

Middle managers face an inherent difficulty in their jobs as a result of their position in the organizational hierarchy. Such people suffer frequently from the problems of conflicting job demands – on the one hand trying to please and win the co-operation of staff whom they supervise, and on the other trying to comply with the demands made by senior management.

They are caught in the middle. An expert on stress, Professor Cary Cooper, believes that this type of situation is one of 'high role conflict'. Research shows that such positions are usually highly stressed. People with high role conflict have been found to have lower job satisfaction and higher job-related tension.

Delegation has many advantages, for example, it enables the planned output to be achieved; the specialist skills of staff are fully used; the manager is freed for planning and innovation; potential in staff is developed and teamwork is strengthened.

Reasons given by managers for not delegating include:

- Managers fear their staff will outshine them
- Managers feel they know they can do the job better than anyone else
- Managers still enjoy the technical aspects of the job from which they were promoted
- Managers like to have lots of things to do (they like to appear busy at all times)
- Manager feels it is easier to do the job himself – quicker than training someone else.

SUCCESSFUL DELEGATION
Delegation takes time to plan. The first step is to analyse

your own job. This can be done in several ways, for example:

- Write a brief description of your own job
- Analyse how you apportion effort now, and how you believe you should apportion it. The following are some typical areas:
  - Spending time with own manager
  - Spending time with colleagues
  - Spending time with staff who report to you
  - Developing self, keeping up to date technically, etc.
  - Short- and long-term planning
  - Customer care: time spent with clients, customers, suppliers
  - Allocating and controlling resources, money, materials, services
  - Monitoring work flow, schedules.

Devise your own list and under each heading ask, for example, the proportion of time taken up by problems thrown up by the system, from your manager, etc.

By making a detailed list and examining it, you can see where your efforts are presently being utilized. You can then go on to list the elements of the job which can be delegated. If, for example, you spend a lot of time in meetings, ask if this is really necessary, could you perhaps send someone else along to represent you?

Consider each of the people who report directly to you, and ask in each case:

- What skills, experience and qualifications he has – those which are used now, or are not used, but could be
- What he does well, and enjoys doing, and is motivated to do

- What you would like him to do, but feel he is not capable of doing right now (Consider training.)
- What he does well, and enjoys doing, but only does through a sense of duty.

Discuss your findings with staff. Ask for their input and keep discussions constructive. Only after discussion can you make the decision as to which member of staff can be delegated specific tasks now, or after further training and experience.

To sum up, the key to effective delegation is a clear understanding of what needs to be done, to which standard and to what time scale by both manger and those who report to him. The appraisal interview is an excellent opportunity for discussion. Outlining job objectives at this time provides a useful vehicle through which tasks can be delegated.

Delegation works most effectively when the manager takes the time to analyse his own situation and style, and to analyse that of those who report to him.

COACHING FOR MOTIVATION

Maslow's 'Hierarchy of Needs' is familiar to many people. Let's briefly look at each of these types of motivational needs in the hierarchical order that Maslow says we seek to satisfy them.

- Self-actualization needs

- Esteem needs

- Social needs

- Safety needs

- Physiological needs

People move up and down the hierarchy

Physiological needs
These are our basic needs which relate to continued survival, such as our need for oxygen, food, sex, sleep, etc. It follows that without these things we will not be too interested in some of the higher motivators!

Safety needs
These are concerned with our need for stability and security. They include such things as our need for routines, law and order, economic and job security.

Social needs
These are related to our need for love and affection, physical contact, family membership, informal social networks, clubs, and organizations.

Esteem needs
These include both the need for self–esteem and the

need for recognition from others. Self-esteem comes from our sense of competence, mastery, and autonomy. Recognition from others comes in the form of praise, status, reputation, etc.

Self-actualization needs
Maslow thought that these were extremely difficult to maintain, and to a certain extent could never be satisfied. He felt that they included such things as our search for truth and justice, and our continuous desire to understand things.

It follows that if any of the lower needs in the hierarchy are not being satisfied, then satisfaction of the upper needs is **not** a compensation.

Some years after Maslow developed his hierarchy, Herzberg developed Maslow's work into his own theory. He classified the different needs into what he called **Satisfiers** (Self-actualization and Esteem) and **Dis-satisfiers** (Physiological, Safety, Social), and further named the Dis-satisfiers as 'Hygiene Factors'.

Dis-satisfiers
These are mainly environment-related, and include

- company policies
- administration (red tape)
- quality of supervision
- physical working conditions
- support systems
- salary, status, job security
- inter-personal relationships.

Increasing these does not necessarily motivate people. Decreasing these, or even playing around with them, will certainly de-motivate people.

Satisfiers
These are mainly work 'content'-related, and include:

- work itself
- achievements
- recognition
- psychological growth.

Increasing these does motivate people, and it also increases the willingness to put up with insufficient physiological, safety and social needs. A competent manager can help boost his own and employee health by providing opportunities to promote 'individual growth'. Research has shown that people work best when they feel that they are performing to the best of their ability, and are given recognition for it.

Coaching can be a rewarding experience for all involved.

Coaching
Coaching is often described as using work assignments to develop skills and potential.

You should make your own lists with the areas which you feel are important to develop staff motivation, but the following checklist will give you some starting points. For each question, ask – 'If not, why not?'

COACHING CHECKLIST

Clear objectives

- Have specific measurable goals been established for each individual reporting to you? ('SMART' objectives)
- Are they up to date?
- Are they challenging?

Delegating effectively

- Have you delegated without 'abdicating'?

- Have you been willing to take risks in permitting those who report to you to perform on their own?

Acknowledged performance

- Have you provided timely praise and recognition for jobs well done?
- Are you specific in expressing your opinions, and feedback?

Provide assistance

- Do you put time aside regularly to review objectives with staff?
- Have you provided suggestions and other assistance when needed by your subordinates?

Rewarding results

- Have financial rewards gone to those members of staff who have produced results – without exception?
- Is there a procedure and policy, known to your staff, for relating rewards to results?

Building confidence

- Have you fostered an effective working relationship with each member of staff?
- Do your staff feel that you have every confidence in them?

Understanding staff

- Do you know the ambitions of each of your members of staff?
- What are the most important motivators for each of them?

Developing

- Do you have a schedule for developmental or coaching contacts with staff, or does it happen at random?

Planning

- Do you have a mutually agreed plan of action for the development of each member of staff, either for the present or for a future job?

Your answers to these questions will provide the basis for your coaching plan.

Example:

Coaching Plan

Employee Name

1. Opportunities:	What tasks could be given as coaching assignments?
2. Choice:	Which new areas of competence does the person need to develop?
3. Targets:	What can realistically be achieved?
4. Timing:	How long will it take?
5. Strategy:	How will you brief and prepare the person for the process?
6. Monitoring:	How will progress be monitored?

The final aspect to consider is – What steps need to be taken to initiate the process?

Well motivated staff are less likely to pass on negative

stress to colleagues. The chain reaction is likely to be a positive experience.

11

DEVELOPING A BALANCED LIFE STYLE

MAIN SOURCES OF STRESS OUTSIDE WORK

Normal anticipated events of life

- Marriage
- Children
- New home
- First home/Change job
- Taxes

Unexpected life events

- Accident
- Death of someone close
- Robbery
- Loss of job
- Unexpected bad news

Progressive accumulating events

- On-going conflict with spouse
- On-going trouble with boss
- Parent-child conflict
- Care of the sick and aged
- Boredom with job/life
- Traffic/noise

Stress builds slowly and increases as a person becomes tired and worn down.

Stressful personal traits

- Perfectionism

- Insecurity
- Incompetence
- Jealousy
- Low self-esteem

These traits can influence the whole day.

Avoid 'Reach back' and 'Play back'
Looking forward and worrying about (as distinct from planning for) events which may never even take place, or letting them reach back from the non-existent future can stress us now. Going over and over again events from the past we can never change, ie. letting them play back like tapes to disturb us emotionally, uses up our nervous energy, distracts us and makes us less effective in what we are doing.

Women and stress

Worried wives most at risk
Bored housewives forced to stay at home to look after children and keep house are likely to be more seriously affected by stress. So says Professor Cary Cooper, a leading stress psychologist from the University of Manchester Institute of Science and Technology, who believes that women suffer twice as many worries as men.

'Just ask who visits the doctor most often for Valium and tranquillizers – it's the housewife,' says Cary. 'It can be very stressful for a woman at home. Doing housework and being responsible for children is hard work, but nowadays there's the dual pressure of housework and a career.'

The unhappy housewife suffers because today many women have high expectations, and she may be frustrated at being trapped in the home. Even the **happy** housewife is sometimes made to suffer and feel guilty because she isn't bringing a wage into the home. In simple terms, she can't win.

'Despite the fact that many women have careers, research shows men still aren't taking responsibility for the housework.' Cooper identifies four types of woman under stress:

1. The housewife who feels trapped by small children and house work.
2. The housewife who enjoys being at home, but feels guilty about it.
3. The working woman who would rather be at home.
4. The working woman whose job is dominated by men.

Dual-career relationships
Here are some tips to deal with this ever increasing type of relationship:

- Discuss what you would like from your work and home lives. Understand the effects your needs have on your partner's freedom of action
- Try to limit your needs so you both have some degree of freedom and an opportunity to cope
- Keep work and home life separate – to reduce conflict
- Make flexible career plans around yourself rather than any organization – be prepared to move, change, retrain
- Share responsibilities for child care, housework etc.

Recent studies indicate that heart attacks among women executives may be on the increase. Women are just as prone to stress-related illnesses as men.

PLANNING
Your lifetime is all you were actually given for making

your way in the world. What you do with the time is what makes your life; what you need is to balance the things you want to do, things that are healthy for you, things you must do to earn your living or pursue your career and things that just give pleasure to you or others. That takes **planning**.

Make a lifetime plan for yourself, always subject to evaluation and adjustment; a statement of your long-term and short-term goals; and day-to-day plan, which includes steps towards accomplishing those goals in addition to daily tasks that must be done.

Here's a sample of such a plan:

Long-term goals

- In the next five years I want to become a senior manager
- In the next five years I want to speak French fluently

Short-term goals

- Call friend
- Have a physical examination
- Update address book
- Clear out dead files

Steps along the way

- Speak with the boss re. future
- Consider advanced academic training in management and finance
- Get business school brochures

To do today

- Meet with my manager
- Get business school brochures
- Call friend (lunch hour)
- Make appointment re. physical

RELAXATION – FIVE WAYS TO BEAT STRESS

Exercise
For on-the-spot relaxation, try the following shoulder exercise:

Find a straight-backed chair and sit down, with the small of your back pressed into the chair. With your tummy tight and upper body lifted, raise both shoulders towards your ears, then slowly relax. Repeat eight times. Now, roll both shoulders backwards, controlling your movements so that you complete eight small circles. Keep your chin level and body lifted. Finally lift both shoulders to your ears, inhale and hold for a count of two. Relax and repeat eight times.

Relaxation therapy

One of the most important methods of dealing with stress is to relieve your inner anger. This simple exercise can be done in the privacy of your bedroom.

Lie on the bed in a darkened room and breathe aggressively, making as much noise as possible. As you breathe in, lift both arms. Then, as you breathe out, slam them down on the bed.

The release of all that anger may leave you in tears, but you'll feel much better for it afterwards.

Meditation

Try this simple meditation exercise: Stop what you are doing and sit on an upright chair. Chose your eyes and count backwards, from 10. As you count, concentrate on your neck muscles, silently telling them to relax. Repeat the exercise until your neck feels comfortable and your mind is calm.

Hypnotherapy

Self-hypnosis has to be taught by a specialist, but anyone can use deep-breathing methods to help them relax. For stress at work, on the train or at home, practise gentle deep-breathing. Breathe in, count to five, hold for a moment, then slowly breathe out. Concentrate on each individual breath, focusing your mind. Repeat the exercise until you feel calm.

Nutrition

Experts advise that stress sufferers should eat frequently, have small meals and avoid stimulants such as tea, coffee and chocolate. Anxiety may cause a drop in your blood-sugar level. Eat plenty of fresh vegetables, fruit, nuts and seeds. And when you are feeling particularly fraught, opt for soothing camomile or rosehip tea.

12

STRESS PREVENTION

THE TEN COMMANDMENTS

I. Plan your day

One of the most stressful things of life today is the feeling that there is never enough time in which to accomplish a job to our complete satisfaction. Everything has to be rushed in an effort to keep up with time, so we become compulsive clock watchers. Time rules, from the alarm in the morning until it is 'time to go to bed'. Why do we allow ourselves to be ruled in this way?

Time is man-made. We devised the system, but we have to continue to manage it if we want to stay healthy. It is essential that we do, because we need the sense of achievement which floods the system when a job is completed to our satisfaction. This is important for the development of pleasure in our work, which in turn gives us the motivation to persevere. If everything has to be rushed there is not only the loss of pleasure in achievement, but also feelings of frustration, anxiety and worry, which are highly stressful. Organization is therefore essential to prevent strain and to give positive feelings of achievement. Make your diary your plan of campaign, e.g. at the time of arranging meetings, agreeing to make presentations, etc. think of the amount of preparation needed and **give yourself sufficient time to prepare**.

Prioritize your daily tasks, starting with the most important. Don't worry if they are not all crossed off at the end of the day. There is another day tomorrow.

2. Give yourself satisfaction

As you accomplish an allotted task during the day, stop

and cross it off the list, savouring the achievement. Only then look at the next priority.

3. Be realistic, you are not superhuman
A little accomplished well is more stress-reducing than a long list of things which you cannot hope to do. Remember that it is the satisfaction of achievement and the positive feedback from this which help to 'stress proof' you for the future.

4. Know your concentration span and energy curve
Everyone's energy curve is different. Some people are wide awake with full high energy first thing in the morning. Others reach their peak at midday and others in the evenings. A good test of this is to suppose that you are working for a very important examination and have no time to study during the day. Would you choose to get up early in the morning, or stay up late at night to do it? Whichever one you would automatically choose is your highest peak. If you have to work on important papers or anything which needs high concentration, work with your own energy curve; you will accomplish better results in less time.

Concentration usually wanders after 45 minutes, so stop then, walk around, rest your eyes and flex your muscles, stretch and relax, then return to the task refreshed. Human performance deteriorates after three hours and then is the time to stop for a light snack and drink. If your work involves mental concentration, try taking some exercise, for example, go for a walk. This will help the flow of blood to the brain and help to dispel the build up of the chemicals of tiredness. Do not begrudge the time to take these breaks – your performance will increase.

5. Learn to delegate
In the home and in the office, spread the load. Don't be too proud to ask for help – people like to feel needed.

6. Try to maintain a balanced system

Allow a reasonable balance between mental activity and physical activity. A good maxim to follow is: when the brain is tired from too much mental effort, take some physical exercise, if only a short walk to restore the balance. When the body is tired, rest it and exercise the mind.

There are natural rhythms of movement and rest which we have learned to ignore because of the needs of our work, our family and all of our responsibilities. Therefore we have to make our own rhythm when and how time permits. This is possible. One can build in physical exercise by walking to the next bus stop or station; by cycling instead of travelling by public transport; by keeping a dog and having to walk it daily. For emotional and physical health keep as fair a balance as possible between physical and mental exercise; between work of any kind, and relaxation; and between activity and sleep. We have rhythmic balances in the body; it is less stressful to work with them rather than against them.

7. Say 'No'

It is mature to say 'no'. Look realistically at your commitments before adding to them. Look also at your allowance of leisure time. Build in some time when you can be free to sit and think, or just sit. To have an action-packed diary may be impressive but it is not realistic in terms of reducing stress.

8. Find something in your work to enjoy

A positive approach to a task, however mundane, gives a lift to the emotions and helps avoid depression. The amount of work done is not as stress-reducing as the manner in which it is done. Never leave the office without a smile and a 'well done' or 'thank you' for someone. It will lift your spirits as well. Go over the day in your mind and find something in it to be pleased about. No one knows exactly what the biochemicals of pleasure are, but they are good and anti-stressful. Positive pleasure is the best tonic in the world and we can prescribe it and give it to ourselves.

9. Laugh to reduce stress

Laughter is a tremendous boost to the system and, along with pleasure, it is an important tonic and antidepressant. Give yourself a little fun every day. Have some music at home which can be relied upon to lift your spirits and lighten your mood. Laughter releases tension and is the quickest stress-reducer there is. It is worth searching out and keeping a store in hand for the really depressing days we all have.

10. Pace yourself

Drive yourself steadily like a Rolls rather than a racing car. A Rolls, we know, needs the right fuel, the right balance of running and resting, and a check-up for any developing major faults every year.

Why not take the same care of yourself? The racing car has a hectic life but a short one; the Rolls has a great life and a longer one.

13

THE FUTURE

The theme of this book has been to help you re-think your approach to stressful situations. If you can reduce stress, for example at work, this will also help reduce stress in other areas of your life.

Planning will help you achieve your long- and short-term goals. Take time out with yourself and the important people in your life to plan for a less stressful lifestyle.

Samuel Butler believed: 'There are two great rules of life, the one general and the other particular. The first is that everyone can, in the end, get what he wants if he only tries. This is the general rule. The particular rule is that every individual is more or less an exception to the general rule.'

I prefer Shirley Conran's view of life:

'Life is too short to stuff a mushroom'

Good Luck!

PERFECT BUSINESS WRITING

Peter Bartram

In every job, writing plays a part – and the ability to write well helps you to perform your job better. Good writing is important both for you and for your organization. It enables you to communicate effectively with your colleagues. It advances your career prospects. It contributes to the success of your company by improving communication with customers and suppliers – and it enhances the corporate image.

If you, like so many people, lack confidence in your writing ability, this book is the perfect answer.

£5.99 Net in the UK only.

ISBN 0-7126-5534-4

PERFECT TIME MANAGEMENT

Ted Johns

Managing your time effectively means adding value to everything you do. This book will help you to master the techniques and skills essential to grasping control of your time and your life.

If you can cut down the time you spend meeting people, talking on the 'phone, writing and reading business papers and answering subordinates' questions, you can use the time saved for creative work and the really important elements of your job. Learn how to deal with interruptions, manage the boss and cut down on meetings time – above all, how to minimize paperwork. You'll be amazed how following a few simple guidelines will improve the quality of both your working life and your leisure time.

£5.99 Net in UK only.

ISBN 0-7126-5549-2

THE PERFECT BUSINESS PLAN

Ron Johnson

A really professional business plan is crucial to success. This book provides a planning framework and shows you how to complete it for your own business in 100 easy to follow stages.

Business planning will help you to make better decisions today, taking into account as many of the relevant factors as possible. A carefully prepared business plan is essential to the people who will put money into the business, to those who will lend it money, and above all to the people who carry out its day to day management.

£5.99 Net in UK only.

ISBN 0-7126-5524-7

THE PERFECT NEGOTIATION

Gavin Kennedy

The ability to negotiate effectively is a vital skill required in business and everyday situations.

Whether you are negotiating over a business deal, a pay rise, a difference of opinion between manager and staff, or the price of a new house or car, this invaluable book, written by one of Europe's leading experts in negotiation, will help you to get a better deal every time, and avoid costly mistakes.

£5.99 Net in UK only.

ISBN 0-7126-5465-8

THE PERFECT PRESENTATION

Andrew Leigh and Michael Maynard

When everything seems to go right, you perform at your absolute best, your audience reacts enthusiastically and comes away inspired, then you've given the perfect presentation!

But success is underpinned by hard work, and the authors of this book provide the necessary framework on which to base your presentations, under the headings of the 'Five Ps': Preparation, Purpose, Presence, Passion and Personality.

Many major organizations have used material from the courses on which this book is based. Now you can gain those benefits – at a fraction of the cost.

£5.99 Net in UK only.

ISBN 0-7126-5536-0

THE PERFECT APPRAISAL

Howard Hudson

Implementing the right appraisal scheme can significantly improve employee and company performance.

Most companies have some form of appraisal scheme in place, yet they get very little out of it. A properly conducted appraisal scheme can raise performance standards, cut costs and in some cases 'revolutionize' the business. This concise and invaluable handbook provides managers and organizations with a practical blueprint for appraisal, and shows how they can obtain maximum benefit from appraisal schemes.

£5.99 Net in UK only
ISBN 0-7126-5541-7

THE PERFECT DISMISSAL

John McManus

Dismissals are wretched occasions for everybody concerned; but unhappiness and unpleasantness can be kept to an absolute minimum by the use of this book.

It tells both employer and employee how to avoid legal pitfalls and their associated costs. Just as importantly, it emphasizes human considerations – common sense, fairness and the dignity of the individual.

The Perfect Dismissal provides a clear and well-balanced summary of a complex subject.

£5.99 Net in UK only.

ISBN 0-7126-5641-3